W9-BXO-992

WILLIAM
TYNDALE

BIBLE TRANSLATOR AND MARTYR

SPECIAL LIVES IN HISTORY THAT BECOME

Signature LIVES

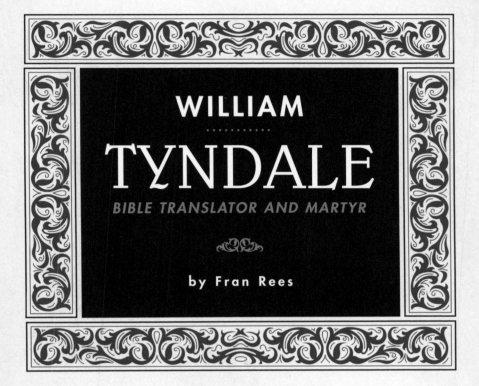

WILLIAM
TYNDALE
BIBLE TRANSLATOR AND MARTYR

by Fran Rees

Content Adviser: C. Mark Steinacher, Th.D.,
Director of Educational Initiatives,
Tyndale University College & Seminary

Reading Adviser: Rosemary G. Palmer, Ph.D.,
Department of Literacy, College of Education,
Boise State University

COMPASS POINT BOOKS ✦ MINNEAPOLIS, MINNESOTA

Compass Point Books
3109 West 50th Street, #115
Minneapolis, MN 55410

Visit Compass Point Books on the Internet at *www.compasspointbooks.com*
or e-mail your request to *custserv@compasspointbooks.com*

Editor: Sue Vander Hook
Page Production: The Design Lab
Photo Researchers: Bobbie Nuyten and Svetlana Zhurkin
Cartographer: XNR Productions, Inc.
Library Consultant: Kathleen Baxter

Art Director: Jaime Martens
Creative Director: Keith Griffin
Editorial Director: Carol Jones
Managing Editor: Catherine Neitge

Quotes from William Tyndale's English Bible have been translated into
modern English for ease of reading.

Library of Congress Cataloging-in-Publication Data
Rees, Fran
   William Tyndale: Bible translator and martyr / by Fran Rees
      p. cm—(Signature lives)
   Includes bibliographical references and index.

ISBN 0-7565-1599-8 (hardcover) 1. Tyndale, William, d. 1536.
2. Reformation—England—Biography. I. Title. II. Series.
   BR350.T8R44 2006
   270.6092—dc22   2005025217

Signature Lives

REFORMATION ERA

The winds of change howled through Europe during the 1500s. The continent that had been united by the Catholic Church found itself in an uproar. In an attempt to reform the church, some people left the established religion, while others worked from within. The changes that began in Germany in 1517 when Martin Luther wrote his *Ninety-Five Theses* would transform everything. The Protestant Reformation's impact would be felt in all aspects of life—at home, in government, and in economics. Straddling the Middle Ages and the Renaissance, the Protestant Reformation would change the church, religion, and the world itself.

Table of Contents

1 BETRAYED

⤬

William Tyndale stepped out of his house and was arrested. His crime was heresy—defying the Roman Catholic Church.

It was May 21, 1535, in Antwerp, Belgium. Tyndale thought he was safe in his sturdy brick home, but he had been betrayed—handed over to the authorities— by his new friend, Henry Phillips.

Phillips seemed like an honest, respectable man. He was from a good English family and had a college degree from Oxford University. But Tyndale didn't know he was actually a man of disgrace and poverty. Just weeks before coming to Antwerp, Phillips was desperate for money. When someone in London, England, approached him about a scheme to make some quick cash, he was more than willing to be part of the plan. His assignment: find and capture William

Engraving from Foxe's Book of Martyrs *shows two men arresting William Tyndale in 1535 outside his home.*

Tyndale, a Roman Catholic priest, translator of the Bible, and now suspected heretic.

When Phillips and Tyndale first met, they discovered they had a lot in common and quickly became friends. On that ill-fated evening in May, Phillips casually stopped by Tyndale's house to ask him for a loan. Tyndale willingly gave him some money, and Phillips offered to take him to dinner. "No, I go forth this day to dinner, and you shall go with me, and be my guest, where you shall be welcome," Tyndale graciously replied.

The two men cheerfully made their way down the long entry of the house toward the door. It was so narrow that only one man could walk along at a time. Tyndale politely motioned for Phillips to go ahead of him. Pretending to show great respect for his friend, Phillips insisted that Tyndale lead the way.

William Tyndale (c. 1494-1536) was a fugitive most of his life.

Tyndale finally gave in and walked ahead of his friend. When he opened the door, two men immediately came into the open. Phillips, who was quite tall, quickly raised his hand over the back of Tyndale's head and pointed at him. This was the man they were looking for.

The officers didn't hesitate to arrest this sought-after priest and take him to prison. They soon took him to a nearby dungeon in the Castle of Vilvorde, where he would stay for more than a year. Leaders of the Roman Catholic Church were pleased that Tyndale had finally been caught. He had been on the run for too long, spreading what they insisted were lies about the church. He believed that salvation came by personal faith in Jesus Christ, not through the church. The Catholic Church, on the other hand, taught that salvation came through the church and by doing good works.

Translating the Bible into English was in direct defiance of the Roman Catholic Church. Tyndale had risked his life so people could read and study the Bible in their own language. He wanted everyone to be able to find what he believed to be the truth in the Holy Scriptures. But this was not what the church wanted. The church thought priests should be the only ones to study the Bible and interpret the message to the masses.

Repeatedly, church leaders visited Tyndale in prison, urging him to recant—take back what he had said about the church. But Tyndale refused. The Bible should be in the language of the common people, he passionately believed. It should not be allowed just in Latin, the only version authorized by the Roman Catholic Church. Highly educated priests and scholars could read Latin. But common people had to rely on the church to teach them what was in the Bible.

Outside the castle, Tyndale's friends worked hard to save him from being condemned to death. His good friend Thomas Poyntz was even willing to risk his own life to save him. Bravely, Poyntz went to government officials in Antwerp and claimed that Tyndale's arrest was illegal. After all, he argued, Tyndale was a citizen of England and exempt from local laws. Poyntz also wrote a letter to his brother John in Essex, England, begging him to ask England's King Henry VIII to help Tyndale.

William Tyndale was taken to a dungeon in the Castle of Vilvorde outside Brussels, Belgium.

John Poyntz made sure his brother's letter was delivered to Thomas Cromwell, the royal secretary to the king. Tyndale should be granted a pardon, Cromwell persuaded the king. Henry agreed it was a good idea to try to save this man. Cromwell wrote two letters to be taken back to Belgium. The letters asked that Tyndale be released, not as a matter of law but as an act of grace. Antwerp officials received the official letters from England, but they refused to release Tyndale. Then they arrested Thomas Poyntz for trying to help him.

Meanwhile, a long investigation of Tyndale began. Because he was not an ordinary prisoner, officials moved along carefully. The main investigator, Pierre Dufief, and others who questioned him had a strong hatred for heretics. They had no tolerance for people who contradicted the teachings of the Roman Catholic Church. Relentlessly, they pressured him to

When William Tyndale lived in Antwerp, Belgium, it was part of the Holy Roman Empire (800–1806). The first title of "king of the Romans" was given to Charlemagne (Charles the Great) (742–814) in 800. At his coronation in Rome, he was crowned by Pope Leo III, head of the Roman Catholic Church. His vast kingdom included present-day France, Switzerland, Belgium, the Netherlands, half of Italy and Germany, and parts of Austria and Spain. A long line of German kings followed as emperor. However, the Protestant Reformation and struggles with the Roman Catholic Church finally weakened the empire, which was scattered and divided by 1648.

renounce his beliefs and embrace the teachings of the church. But Tyndale stood fast to what he believed to be God's truths. He would not recant.

In August 1536, nearly 15 months after his arrest, Tyndale was charged, tried, and found guilty of heresy. His penalty was a cruel death—burning at the stake. But first, church officials conducted a ceremony to rid him of his rights as a priest. His hands were scraped to symbolically remove the sacred oil that had been applied when he was anointed a priest. The holy sacraments—the bread and the wine given at communion—were placed in his hands and then removed. Then he was condemned and further stripped of his priestly position.

"We commit your soul to the devil," echoed the final condemnation. Then the church turned Tyndale over to the local court system. For the next two months, his fellow Catholic priests again tried to persuade him to return to the beliefs of the church. Time and again, Tyndale refused.

Finally, on October 6, 1536, Tyndale was stripped of nearly all his clothing and bound with chains. He was taken out of his prison dungeon to a public place, where citizens of Antwerp could gather and watch. There he was tied to a wooden stake. Bundles of sticks and larger pieces of wood were piled at the bottom. According to custom, he was given a few moments to pray before his death. As the executioner

William Tyndale was strangled before his body was burned, which was considered an act of mercy.

tightened a rope around his neck and prepared to strangle him, Tyndale cried out in a loud voice, "Lord, open the king of England's eyes."

As a final act of mercy, the executioner pulled the rope tight and strangled Tyndale. The fire was lit

William Tyndale died for translating the Bible into English so common people could read and study it themselves.

beneath him, and his body burned to ashes. When the fire cooled down, his ashes were scooped up and thrown into the river. People believed the ashes of heretics should not be left to dirty the earth.

William Tyndale was about 42 years old when he

died for what he believed in. His life and his death would impact the world for hundreds of years to come. The Bible he translated into English would later inspire the widely read English version of the Bible—the 1611 Authorized King James Version. The eloquent prose in Tyndale's translation became some of the most well-known and most-quoted words in the English language.

Tyndale came to be called the Father of the English Bible. He is also remembered as a man extremely dedicated to God who gave his life to provide the Holy Scriptures to English-speaking people. There is no indication that he ever wavered in his faith. He stood firm in his beliefs—even to the point of martyrdom. In the 16th-century book, *Foxe's Book of Martyrs*, author John Foxe gave William Tyndale a fitting title—the "good martyr of God."

2 Extraordinary Student

No one knows exactly where William Tyndale was born. It was somewhere near Slimbridge, Gloucestershire, England, near the border of Wales. No one is sure about the date of his birth, either. But it was probably in about 1494. The first names of his parents are unknown. His family name was first said to be Hutchins; sometimes it was also spelled Hutchyns, Hychyns, or Hewchuns. Later, it was revealed that the family name was actually Tindale, also spelled Tyndale or Tyndal.

The family was descended from Hugh de Tindale, baron of Langley Castle in Northumberland, England. The story goes that Hugh de Tindale fled to the south from Northumberland during the Wars of the Roses (1455–1487) and changed his name to Hutchins for safety. On his deathbed, however, he revealed to his

William Tyndale grew up near Berkeley Castle in Gloucestershire, England.

children that his true name was Tindale.

Young William spent his childhood in the Vale of Berkeley, a lush rural area of England in the gentle hills called the Cotswolds. There were quiet valleys full of crops and sheep. Clear streams ran through the hills. Attractive stone buildings nestled among the green fields. Gardens blooming with flowers trimmed the sturdy, well-planned houses.

As a young boy, William may have climbed up Stinchcombe Hill and looked out over the hills and valleys that stretched far away into several counties. In the distance towered Berkeley Castle, where England's King Edward II had been killed in 1327.

William belonged to a large family that was highly respected locally and well-known even in London. They were wealthy and influential. William's brothers, Edward and John, were powerful businessmen in the area. Edward was the collector of the crown rents, an important government position that made sure citizens paid a type of English tax. John organized the sale of cloth in the area and in London.

In the Vale of Berkeley, people were proud of the region's lively trade in wool and other cloth. Weekly cloth markets in the area drew people from far and near. There were plenty of local fairs and events to keep people busy and entertained.

About half the population worked in the cloth industry. Men, women, and children spent hours each day raising sheep, shearing them for wool, spinning thread, and preparing the finished cloth. Wool cloth was then taken to local, national, and international markets, where it was used to make clothing, blankets, and other goods. People in many different professions were needed to produce and sell all the cloth that was made in the area. There were shepherds, shearers, carriers, market officials, wool merchants, mill owners, spinners, weavers, dyers, and more.

Sixteenth-century illustration of sheep shearers shows how farmers in the Vale of Berkeley got their wool, which was spun into thread and made into cloth.

Even though William lived in rural England, it was not cut off from the rest of the world. Several trade and travel routes connected the area to many other parts of England. William learned much about the world from a variety of people who traveled throughout the region.

He heard people speaking many different languages when he was growing up. In addition to his own native English, William was used to hearing the melodious Welsh language spoken by the people in the nearby country of Wales. In school, he learned Latin and became familiar with many other dialects, or versions, of English. Living on a trade route gave him opportunities to learn many things.

William was an extraordinary student and took advantage of the excellent education available at his grammar school called Wotton-under-Edge. Languages came easily for him, and by the age of 10, he could read Latin.

Oxford University in Oxford, England, is the oldest English-speaking university in the world. Teaching at Oxford began as early as 1096. It rapidly developed after 1167, when England's King Edward II banned English students from attending the University of Paris. Bible translator John Wycliffe (c. 1320-1384) attended Oxford University more than 130 years before William Tyndale studied there. Wycliffe worked to translate parts of the Bible into the language of the common people and often challenged the teachings of the Roman Catholic Church. After his death, the Catholic Church declared him a heretic, dug up his body, and burned his remains. Wycliffe's followers were called Lollards.

A typical grammar school in 16th-century England

By the age of 12, William was finished with grammar school. He left the beautiful farm country of Gloucestershire and went to the city of Oxford, England, to attend Oxford University. As a college student, he would blossom into a talented, hardworking scholar. ✍

3 UNIVERSITY SCHOLAR

—∞—

William Tyndale attended college with about 1,000 other students at Oxford University, all of them boys. He lived in one of the small dormitories, called houses or homes, with about 20 other students. The boys in each house formed a kind of family, with everyone eating together in a central hall and living on the same schedule.

Along with his classmates, William rose every day at 5 A.M. for a religious Roman Catholic service before the morning lecture at 6 A.M. A bell or horn sounded at about 11 A.M. to announce the first meal of the day. Another bell rang later at 5 P.M. for evening supper. Before going to bed, students sang a religious chant, a song in Latin using just one or two musical tones. The atmosphere was one of family, studies, and religious worship.

Most graduates of Oxford University became priests in the Roman Catholic Church.

King's College at Cambridge University was founded in 1441 by England's King Henry VI. Tyndale attended Cambridge after his studies at Oxford.

William spoke only Latin at the university. He was not allowed to speak his native English, since it was looked down upon for well-educated scholars to speak anything but Latin. It was the required language at Oxford. Students could only speak English in the halls during feasts and holidays.

According to William, the classes at Oxford

were dull and unchallenging. He thought students should be allowed to think more freely. Most of his classes were about religion and the Bible, and he often disagreed with what his teachers taught. But he finished his classes and graduated with a Bachelor of Arts degree on July 4, 1512. Three years later, he earned his Master of Arts degree.

In 1516, William went to Cambridge, England, where he attended Cambridge University for further studies in religion. There he studied Greek, the language of the original New Testament portion of the Bible. It wasn't long before he was able to read the New Testament in Greek. William met many students and teachers at Cambridge who discussed new ways of thinking about life and religion.

Tyndale was living during a time when the world was changing in many ways. Ever since Johannes Gutenberg finished his printing press in the 1450s, knowledge and books had spread throughout Europe more quickly than ever before in history. Printing workshops had sprung up all over Europe. Thinkers and writers could

In the 1450s, Johannes Gutenberg (c. 1398–1468) finished his printing press. Books could now be mass-produced instead of individually handwritten. The first book ever printed using the printing press was the Bible in Latin, often called Gutenberg's Bible. Printing brought with it the ability for new religious and social ideas to spread rapidly throughout Europe. People clamored to read, and books sold quickly.

Johannes Gutenberg's mass printing of the Latin Bible paved the way for the printing of 10 million books over the next 45 years.

now print and sell books on many different subjects. More and more people were reading books filled with facts and information they had never known before.

This period of time came to be called the Renaissance, a word that means *rebirth*. It was a new beginning of ideas, art, science, and exploration. Many new ideas were exchanged about religion, and people started questioning what they had always been taught by their religious leaders. People also started striving for excellence in many areas. The new thinkers of the Renaissance—or the Renaissance man, as individuals were called—encouraged people to develop their human abilities to the fullest and expand their learning in all subjects.

Even religious leaders had new ideas during this

period. Some of them dared to disagree with and criticize the teachings and traditions of the centuries-old Roman Catholic Church. Some even questioned the church's supreme leader, the pope. Mass printing allowed them to spread their teachings to a lot of people and build a following of others who agreed with them. The Catholic Church didn't approve of people who questioned the church or tried to radically change it. Some reformers were arrested and tried for heresy. Their punishment was death, usually by burning at the stake. This religious movement came to be called the Protestant Reformation.

John Wycliffe (c. 1320–1384) was an early supporter of reform in the Roman Catholic Church.

At Cambridge, Tyndale met many religious reformers, especially those who were influenced by a group in England called the Lollards. This group followed the teachings of John Wycliffe who had translated portions of the Bible into English. Lollards wandered about the English countryside preaching that changes should be made in the Roman Catholic Church. As a result, they were severely persecuted and punished in England. Many of them had been burned at the stake for their beliefs.

In the early 1500s, a German Catholic priest named Martin Luther also began preaching against the principles of the Roman Catholic Church. Luther disagreed with the sale of indulgences, official documents signed by the pope that promised the forgiveness of sins. Church leaders were teaching that people could pay money for their spiritual salvation. They could even pay to have the sins of dead relatives forgiven.

In 1517, Martin Luther began lecturing at Wittenberg University in Wittenberg, Germany. The door of Castle Church there was a kind of bulletin board, where professors and students posted topics they wanted to discuss. When Luther nailed his 95 complaints against the Roman Catholic Church to the church door, he didn't plan to start a religious revolution. His intent was to stir debate.

In 1517, the year after Tyndale went to Cambridge University, Luther posted a list of 95 complaints against the Roman Catholic Church. He nailed them to the door of the church at Wittenberg in eastern Germany. They came to be called Luther's *Ninety-Five Theses*.

Tyndale agreed with many of these new religious ideas that were being discussed. He shared some of the ideas of the Lollards and agreed with Luther in many ways. In spite of his questions and doubts about the church, he was ordained, or officially appointed, a Roman Catholic priest in 1521. But

Martin Luther nailed his complaints against the Roman Catholic Church to the door of Castle Church in Wittenberg, Germany, in 1517.

he would be a priest in name only. He never served as a priest in a Catholic Church.

In 1522, Tyndale left Cambridge. He was about 27 years old. It was time to move on and get a job. He returned to the English countryside to become a tutor at the home of John Walsh, a Gloucestershire landowner. But he didn't leave his new ideas and his changing beliefs at Cambridge. What he learned there had altered his thinking and would affect him for the rest of his life. ✑

"A Boy That Driveth the Plough"

Chapter 4

As teacher for the oldest child of Sir John and Lady Anne Walsh, William Tyndale was treated as a member of the family. He lived with them in their large house of soft gray stone that stood majestically in the middle of lawns and trees. Built around an inner courtyard of plants and flowers, the Walsh estate included a fine great hall and a private chapel where religious services were held.

Tyndale taught reading, Latin, and other subjects to 7-year-old Maurice Walsh. Because his teaching duties were not too time-consuming, he had plenty of time to follow his passion for debate and preaching. He often preached at the Walsh chapel and at churches in the area.

Sometimes preachers spoke outside in public areas called commons or greens. All who passed by on the streets could hear them. Preachers also walked from town to town or rode on horseback throughout the countryside. Sometimes they spoke in churchyards and sometimes in an open field. John Wycliffe was one of the first "Bible men," as these traveling preachers were called. They believed in a simple life. Often they were poor and dressed in modest, drab clothing.

Even though these men preached in English, the only Bible allowed by the Roman Catholic Church in England was the Latin Vulgate. Since common people couldn't read Latin, the Bible remained a mystery to

John Wycliffe sends his band of traveling preachers out to teach from his English translation of parts of the Latin Vulgate Bible.

them. They relied on the Catholic Church to tell them about God and salvation.

When Tyndale preached out-doors in public places, he spoke with force and passion. His ideas about salvation and the church often shocked and angered other Catholic clergy in the Gloucestershire area. The more dignified priests did not go to hear Tyndale's open-air sermons. They learned of his ideas from other people or even at conversations over the dinner table at the Walsh home. The Walshes often held grand dinners in the great hall

In 382, Pope Damascus I commissioned a priest named Jerome (c. 347–420) to translate the Bible from Hebrew and Greek into Latin. The task took him 20 years to complete. This Bible came to be known as the versio vulgata *(common translation) and became the only accepted version in the Catholic Church. It is still used by the church and commonly known as the* Vulgate.

at their estate. They invited priests, well-educated people, and the rich to dine and talk.

Tyndale was also invited to these dinners. He was not afraid to challenge some of the ideas of the Walshes' most highly respected guests. Tyndale would win many arguments with them by producing the Latin Vulgate Bible and proving from certain passages that they were wrong. Because they were guests of the Walshes, these rich, educated men could not be openly rude to Tyndale. Instead, they waited until they left and talked about him to people outside of the Walsh home. At times, they invited the Walshes to their own banquets, where they felt free to speak quite openly against Tyndale and his radical religious ideas.

Lady Walsh was impressed that such important men found her son's teacher to be challenging and even dangerous. But she confronted Tyndale and asked him why she should believe him instead of those wealthy and accomplished men. Still somewhat young and inexperienced in his profession, Tyndale could not defend himself completely.

In order to win the respect of the family, he translated a book from Latin into English. The author of the book was a man named Desiderius Erasmus,

William Tyndale was a private tutor at Manor House in Little Sodbury, England, kept by Sir John Walsh.

a well-known Renaissance writer. In his book, titled *The Christian Soldier's Handbook,* Erasmus stressed that a true Christian has knowledge of the Scriptures. He claimed that people could find all they needed in the Bible. Erasmus also was critical of what he believed to be greed and false beliefs within the Roman Catholic Church.

The Walshes were impressed with Tyndale's translation, and they agreed with many of Erasmus' ideas. They began to defend Tyndale's arguments and did not invite critical people to their home as often. When negative people did visit, the Walshes were not as friendly to them as they had been in the past. After a while, these rich men of learning and importance no longer came to their manor. Instead, they began to plan their revenge against Tyndale. They accused him of heresy and planned a way to force him to appear before Chancellor John Bell, a high-ranking government official.

Bell was a harsh man, and Tyndale was afraid of him. He had no way to prepare for a hearing before

Erasmus finished his version of the Greek New Testament in 1516.

this powerful man. No formal charges were made against Tyndale, but he knew his life might be in danger if he were linked with the rebellious and much hated Lollards. Tyndale certainly did not want to put his life at risk, but he refused to deny the beliefs and ideas he held so strongly.

At the hearing, Tyndale demanded to know who had brought evidence against him. None of his accusers stepped forward. Instead, the chancellor threatened him and scolded him. Tyndale spoke up, insisting that his beliefs and ideas were the same as those stated in the New Testament. He was only speaking the truth from the Bible, he claimed. Since there was no one to testify against him, Tyndale was released with only a stern warning from Bell.

Pope Leo X was the leader of the Roman Catholic Church from 1513 until his death in 1521.

Tyndale continued to speak out and criticize the Roman Catholic Church and even the pope. In one argument, he said he believed only in God's laws, and he defied the pope and all his laws. He promised the pope, "If God spare my life, before many years I will cause a boy that driveth the plough, shall know more of the scripture than thou dost." In other words, common people would know as much about the Scriptures as religious leaders.

This insult to the pope was reported to all the Roman Catholic churches in the area. Church leaders began to investigate this tutor and priest for possible charges of heresy. Concerned over the turmoil he had stirred up and the harm that might come to the Walsh family because of him, Tyndale decided to leave his job and move to London.

In July 1523, he arrived in London with a letter of introduction from Walsh and a dream to translate the Bible into English. He was about 28 years old, an unemployed teacher and priest with no money, no support, and no friends. He was,

> *The pope is the supreme head of the Roman Catholic Church. He governs the church from Vatican City, a tiny independent country within the city of Rome, Italy. The word pope comes from the Greek word pappas, which is a child's name for father. The Catholic Church believes that certain statements made by the pope are infallible—without error—on matters of faith and morals.*

however, a brilliant scholar and linguist, a man with an incredible talent for languages. He would eventually learn to read and speak eight languages: English, French, German, Hebrew, Greek, Latin, Italian, and Spanish.

But for now, he hoped to find someone in London to support his grand project. Who better, he thought, than the powerful and learned bishop of London, Cuthbert Tunstall? He had the authority to authorize an English translation of the Bible. He also had a beautiful palace, where Tyndale hoped to live and work on his translation.

First, Tyndale took his letter of introduction to Sir Henry Guildford, an influential man who could convince Tunstall to meet with him. The bishop had very little time, however, for an obscure young man from a small faraway village. But after many months, Tyndale was given a short meeting with the bishop, and he presented his plan to him.

The meeting did not go well, however. Tyndale was awkward, nervous, and unprepared. The bishop turned him away, saying he was too busy and suggested that Tyndale look somewhere else for support. Under the circumstances, the bishop was quite polite. He could have been much harsher with Tyndale. After all, Tyndale was proposing to translate the Bible into English, a crime that had been punishable by death in England for more than 100 years.

Even though the bishop had been courteous, Tyndale was angry. He was passionate about one thing—providing all English-speaking people with the Holy Scriptures in their own language. Instead of being grateful for the polite refusal from the bishop, he attacked Tunstall in letters and conversations. He was furious that the bishop would deny the citizens of England a chance to read about salvation for themselves in the Bible.

Cuthbert Tunstall (1474–1559) was the Roman Catholic bishop in charge of the London area.

It was no secret that Tunstall and his good friend, Sir Thomas More, hated heresy. Neither one tolerated people who went against the traditions and teachings of the Roman Catholic Church. Tyndale probably knew that these men would not support his cause, but he didn't know that they would one day be responsible for hunting him down and charging him with a crime punishable by death.

The encounter with Tunstall didn't discourage Tyndale, however, and he continued to pursue his dream. He immediately started looking for others

Some wealthy merchants in London, England, supported Tyndale financially.

who might support his cause. Finally, he found one man who agreed to help him—a man named Humphrey Monmouth, a kind and wealthy cloth merchant. Monmouth was part of a secret ring of London merchants who agreed with some of the new religious ideas coming out of Germany. Most of these ideas were based on Martin Luther's religious teachings and beliefs.

For six months, Tyndale lived in Monmouth's house. During that time, he convinced Monmouth and some of his friends to give him money for his project. But their help was not enough. In early 1524, Tyndale left London, declaring that "there was no room in my lord of London's palace to translate the New Testament, but also that there was no place to do it in all England." In April, he sailed for Hamburg, Germany, where he would begin to translate the New Testament. ✑

5 FUGITIVE TRANSLATOR

In Germany, at about the age of 29, William Tyndale began his life's work. By now, he knew he had to do his work secretly. Where he was and what he did during the next few years is not known completely. He was never able to stay in one city for very long. Alert, strong-minded, practical, and dedicated, Tyndale began studying and translating.

For 11 years, he skillfully moved from city to city in Europe, translating the Bible and fulfilling his dream of making the Scriptures available to the common people. Determined to escape those who wanted to arrest him, he found help along the way from people who agreed with his religious ideas. Whenever he felt in danger of being caught, he would flee to another city.

During those years, Tyndale never returned to

Cologne, Germany, was one of many cities where Tyndale hid in order to avoid arrest.

England. Thomas More and others actively hunted for him for at least nine of the 11 years. Tyndale figured out clever ways to dodge anyone who searched for him. He knew that what he was doing was punishable by death, but he would not let anything stop him from accomplishing the work to which he was intensely dedicated. Living alone as a fugitive, he must have decided he didn't want to put family and friends through the dangers that he faced.

Meanwhile, in May 1524, when Tyndale arrived in Hamburg, Germany, the Reformation was at its peak. Seven years before, Martin Luther had nailed his *Ninety-Five Theses* to the church door at Wittenberg. A group had formed that was soon labeled Protestants, which stood for protesters. They were speaking out against what they thought were the wrong-doings and false doctrines of the Roman Catholic Church.

Martin Luther (1483-1546) is considered the Father of the Protestant Reformation.

Tyndale and Luther met each other in Germany, but how much they shared their ideas or discussed their goals and plans is not known.

Tyndale learned German in just a few months. He wanted to be able to read and refer to Luther's German translation of the New Testament while he worked on his English translation. He also used Erasmus' Latin translation of the New Testament and the Latin Vulgate version used by the Roman Catholic Church. Next to the text of the Bible, Tyndale added some of his own comments to explain his views and beliefs. He also wrote and published religious pamphlets and booklets. He hired a man named William Roye to be his secretary. Roye took dictation and copied

Disguised as a knight, Martin Luther hid from officials of the Roman Catholic Church to start his German translation of the Bible.

manuscripts for Tyndale.

In April 1525, Tyndale finished his first English translation of the New Testament, probably while living in the city of Wittenberg, Germany. Then he and Roye left for Cologne, Germany, to find a printer who would publish it. Would he be able to find a printer there who would be willing to risk his life to print the English New Testament?

Cologne is located at the intersection of the Rhine River and one of the major trade routes between eastern and western Europe. Today, it is the fourth largest city in Germany. It is considered the economic, cultural, and historical capital of the region.

Tyndale and Roye were somewhat safe in Cologne, since it was a busy trading city. They could come and go without being noticed or causing any alarm or excitement. But it was a dangerous time, especially for printers who dared to print controversial materials. Tyndale had to find a printer who was willing to take the risk and whom he could trust to keep his secret. Peter Quentel was the man. Soon, Tyndale made arrangements with him to print 6,000 copies of his New Testament. He paid Quentel with money from supporters in England.

Trouble lay ahead for Quentel, however. John Dobneck, a devout Roman Catholic, overheard some of the workers from Quentel's print shop bragging about Tyndale's English Bible as they drank wine.

Tyndale checks a printed page of his English translation of the New Testament at a print shop in Cologne, Germany, in 1525.

They said it was going to cause trouble in England for the Roman Catholic Church and the king. Wanting to learn more, Dobneck bought the workers dinner and more wine. He soon found out many details about Tyndale's project. The newly printed English Bibles were going to be shipped secretly to England, he discovered, and the whole project was being paid for by wealthy English merchants. Dobneck immediately went to city authorities in Cologne to convince them to stop the project. They decided to act—they would raid the print shop and stop the printing.

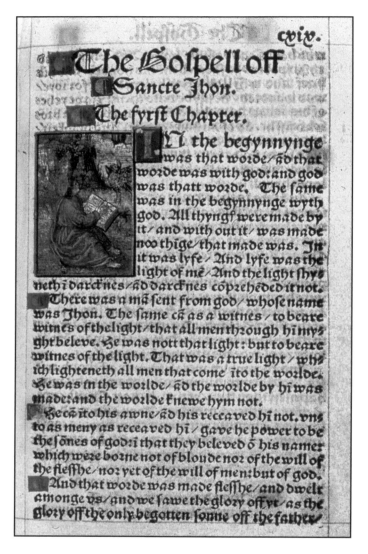

Just before the raid, someone tipped off Tyndale. Quickly, he stopped the printing and escaped with Roye by boat up the Rhine River. They headed to the city of Worms, Germany. But before they left, Tyndale hurriedly grabbed some of the printed sheets of the Bible to take with him.

In England, King Henry VIII was told about the printing of English Bibles. He was advised to keep a close watch on all English ports in case Tyndale tried to ship Bibles to England. Now safely in Worms, Tyndale and Roye found themselves where many of Luther's supporters also lived. For now, the Englishmen were safe.

Soon, Tyndale hired another printer, a man named Peter Schöffer, to print another edition of his New Testament. Tyndale and Roye spent most of their waking hours at the print shop, supervising the workmen and getting the presses ready. Less than six months after they arrived in Worms, finished copies were being loaded onto barges and shipped down the Rhine River on their way to England. There is no record of exactly how many copies of the Worms edition were printed, but it is believed there were as many as 6,000 copies. Not a word about the printing leaked out until all the copies were completed.

Excitement in England rose

Much of Peter Schöffer's printing equipment had belonged to Johannes Gutenberg, the inventor of the printing press. In 1455, Schöffer and his partner, Johann Fust, sued Gutenberg for an unpaid debt. Gutenberg lost the lawsuit and had to give his printing press and equipment to Fust and Schöffer. Tyndale's New Testament may have been printed with some of Gutenberg's printing equipment.

over the chance to read the Bible in English. Bibles shipped to England from Germany were costly, but people were willing to pay a high price for them. Not only were people eager to read the Bible, they were also excited about the beautiful language Tyndale used to translate the text. His translation of the prose was simple and forceful; it appealed to people of all walks of life.

The title page of Tyndale's English translation of the New Testament shows the ornate Gothic letters typically used in the 16th century.

Later, Tyndale's language was verified as an accurate translation of the Bible. The language was easy to understand. It flowed in a pleasant, rhythmical way. The beauty of his phrases is unforgettable to many people. A Scripture passage from I Corinthians

in the New Testament reads:

> *When I was a child, I spake as a child, I*
> *imagined as a child: but as soon as I was*
> *a man I put away childishness.*

In the same passage, the words are plain, lyrical, and inspiring:

> *Love suffereth long and is courteous. Love*
> *envieth not ... dealeth not dishonestly,*
> *seeketh not her own, ... believeth all things,*
> *hopeth all things, endureth in all things. ...*
> *love falleth never away.*

Tyndale wrote the familiar English version of the Lord's Prayer much as it is still known today:

> *O our father which art in heaven,*
> *   hallowed be thy name.*
> *Let thy kingdom come; thy will be fulfilled*
> *   as well in earth as it is in heaven.*
> *Give us this day our daily bread*
> *And forgive us our trespasses, even as we*
> *   forgive them which trespass us,*
> *Lead us not into temptation, but deliver*
> *   us from evil.*

Tyndale was very humble about his work. In his preface, the introductory section of his New Testament, he asked his readers to forgive him if his English offended them in any way. He promised that he had not used anyone else's English translations but that the words they read were his own translation.

Some of the words and phrases Tyndale used in his translation made the Roman Catholic Church very angry. His translation stated that Jesus Christ's body was the congregation, any group of people who believed in Jesus. The Catholic Church, however, believed that Christ's body was the Roman Catholic Church and, more particularly, the pope and the priests of the church. What Tyndale wrote completely contradicted the church's teachings. The church had no doubt about it—Tyndale was a heretic.

Tyndale's translation of the New Testament was becoming more and more popular. Printers in cities outside Worms wanted to print it. A printer in Antwerp even stole a copy and printed it himself. By August 1526, so many of Tyndale's translations were being printed and shipped to England that an emergency meeting of England's Roman Catholic bishops was called. These church leaders wanted to punish anyone who transported, sold, or even read these English Bibles.

On October 23, 1526, Bishop Tunstall made a proclamation about people who translated the Bible into any language but Latin or agreed with the ideas of Martin Luther. They were children of sin, he said, blinded by extreme wickedness, and wanderers from the truth. He accused Tyndale of spreading poison

By the 1500s, thousands of print shops like this early shop had spread throughout Europe.

throughout London. All copies of the English version of the New Testament must be seized within 30 days, Tunstall demanded. Those who did not obey and turn in their Bibles would be excommunicated— completely excluded and removed from the Roman Catholic Church. They would also be fully investigated on suspicion of heresy.

Tunstall went even further and ordered that seized Bibles be burned. Many were shocked that anyone would destroy the Holy Scriptures. People claimed that the real heresy was in the burning of the Bibles, not in the translating of them.

On Sunday, October 28, 1526, Tunstall gathered the Bibles he had seized and brought them to

English translations of the Bible were burned in London to prevent ordinary people from reading them.

St. Paul's Cathedral in London. There he preached a fiery sermon, accusing Tyndale of writing a strange doctrine. After criticizing Tyndale's New Testament for having thousands of errors, Tunstall burned every copy of the seized Bibles.

In spite of the danger, Tyndale continued to pursue his life's work. English Bibles were still being printed in Germany and Belgium. There was power in the printed word, he believed. Many people in England were willing to risk their memberships in the Roman Catholic Church and pay large sums of money for the chance to read the Bible in English. Those who could not read were inspired to learn just so they could read the Bible and understand the religious pamphlets and posters that were pouring off the presses.

The more people demanded Bibles, the angrier the Roman Catholic clergy became. Tyndale had to become even more secretive about his whereabouts. But even as he moved from city to city, somehow he continued to oversee the printing and the smuggling of thousands of Bibles. ❧

Chapter

6 God's Smuggler

Tyndale's goal was not only to translate and print the Bible but also to get those translations into the hands of as many people as possible, as quickly as possible. Tyndale cleverly had some translations printed in small sizes with paper covers. Small, soft books were easier to smuggle and pass from person to person. He arranged for these small Bibles to be hidden on boats going to England. They were delivered to obscure docks, unloaded, and carefully passed along to people who would risk their lives to deliver and sell them. Copies were being sold secretly by early spring of 1526.

Because of Tyndale's secrecy, no one knows exactly who helped him or how he arranged for the Bibles to be shipped to England. But it is known that money and help came from some English merchants

People were eager to read English Bibles that were smuggled into England.

living in England, Belgium, and Germany. Bibles were tucked into bales of cloth and other merchandise. They were loaded onto boats and carried along waterways in and around London. Bibles arrived in England—thousands of them.

As time went on, the business of printing, selling, and smuggling Bibles became more dangerous. Booksellers in England were warned not to sell Tyndale's New Testament. This was not the only religious book that was banned. Five years earlier, in 1521, Roman Catholic Cardinal Thomas Wolsey had banned all of Martin Luther's books and any publication that supported the Protestant Reformation. Catholic bishops in England and Wales read Wolsey's order in every Catholic Church in the land to give church members fair warning.

For the most part, printers in England followed Wolsey's order. But printers in the rest of Europe— especially in Germany, France, and Belgium—kept on printing and shipping Luther's books and pamphlets, openly defying the ban. When books continued to arrive in England from other parts of Europe, Sir Thomas More was outraged. By now, he had become an outspoken enemy of Tyndale and Luther.

Smuggling of items was not a new practice in England. Along the North Sea coast, smuggling had thrived for more than 100 years. People regularly smuggled goods so they wouldn't have to pay taxes

In western Europe, a traveling bookseller offers a book to his customer.

or customs duties. Smugglers made fortunes getting items like wool, cloth, wine, and spices in and out of England. English beer was smuggled out in barrels by passing it off as drinking water. Smugglers bribed English officials, who were supposed to watch the ports and stop the illegal transporting of goods. The business of smuggling flourished, and English merchants were skilled at bypassing government taxes.

London and other English cities along the Thames River were perfect places for smugglers to ship and receive hidden cargo. Isolated creeks and quiet inlets, along with islands and remote shores, were perfect spots to load and unload illegal goods onto small boats.

Books were not subject to taxes or customs, but only certain people were given a license to import, sell, or publish them in English. Others who did so without a license were punished severely. They were put in prison, all their belongings were seized, and their families were left in poverty.

Smuggling English Bibles was even more dangerous, because they were now considered illegal. One printer and bookseller was arrested in London and died in prison for printing Tyndale's Bibles. In Germany, printers were being put to death for the crime of printing works written by Luther.

Still, the smuggling continued. Instead of always hiding complete Bibles, flat printed sheets were

Tyndale smuggled English Bibles into the London port, but he also used many smaller ports to avoid authorities who were on the lookout for them.

sometimes hidden with other cargo, mixed in with cloth, paper, glassware, wines, or food. Printed Bibles were hidden in barrels and labeled "wine" or "oil" or something else. Sometimes they were tucked into sacks of flour or laid inside boxes of furs.

Letters, papers, and cash from Tyndale's supporters were stowed in hidden compartments inside chests or in bales of cloth. So smugglers knew where to find the hidden cargo, containers with Bibles and papers were marked with a dab of color or a twist of cloth. Thomas More was able to find and seize some of the illegal Bibles, but most of them got through to the people of England.

Angry because they couldn't stop the selling of English Bibles, leaders in the Roman Catholic Church and government officials in London tried to stop printers in other countries from printing them. Bishop Tunstall went to Antwerp and promised to pay a cloth merchant named Packington a lot of money for every copy he delivered to him personally. Packington, who happened to be one of

Smuggling Bibles did not end in the 16th century. For hundreds of years, Bibles have been carried secretly into countries where they are illegal. In the mid-1950s, a man who called himself Brother Andrew began smuggling thousands of Bibles into the Soviet Union and Eastern Europe on numerous trips in his old Volkswagen. In 1981, a million Bibles were smuggled into China. Millions more Bibles were later delivered to Latin America, North Korea, and other countries.

John Frith (1503-1533) was imprisoned for helping William Tyndale translate the Bible into English. He was later convicted of heresy and burned at the stake.

Tyndale's friends, told Tyndale about the encounter. He told Tyndale that someone was willing to buy every unsold copy of his work.

When Tyndale asked who the man was, Packington didn't hesitate to tell him. It was the bishop of London. Tyndale knew why Tunstall wanted the Bibles—he wanted to burn them.

Perhaps for financial reasons, Packington accepted Tunstall's offer and agreed to deliver the English Bibles.

Tyndale commented:

> *Well, I am the gladder, for these two ben-*
> *efits shall come thereof: I shall get money*
> *of him for these books, to bring myself out*
> *of debt, and the whole world shall cry out*
> *upon the burning of God's word.*

Packington did what he promised and delivered the Bibles to Tunstall. The bishop burned them all. Tyndale used the money to pay off his debts and make corrections to his New Testament. Soon he began printing another edition. ஒ

7 ENEMIES IN HIGH PLACES

❧⟨✺⟩❧

Some very important people in England were getting angrier with William Tyndale. By distributing his Bibles and speaking out about his beliefs, Tyndale was going against some of the most powerful leaders of the Roman Catholic Church and the government of England. His worst enemies were Bishop Tunstall, Cardinal Wolsey, and Thomas More.

Tunstall was a clergyman, but he was also a lawyer, a diplomat, and a politician. As bishop, he was the top Roman Catholic leader for all of London. He had the power to allow the distribution of Tyndale's New Testament, if he wanted. But he was fearless in his pursuit of heretics or anyone who disagreed with the Roman Catholic Church. He believed that Tyndale was an enemy of the church, and he had no tolerance for him.

Thomas More disagreed with William Tyndale over many issues and became one of Tyndale's greatest enemies.

Tunstall had known Tyndale wanted to translate the Bible ever since they first met in 1523. He certainly didn't know then, however, that Tyndale would accomplish his dream just three years later. Although Tyndale never put his name on his translations, Tunstall knew who the translator was. He vowed to stop him.

Tyndale's problems didn't stop with Tunstall, however. He also had to deal with More, who criticized and pursued him constantly. This English politician and staunch Catholic became Tyndale's worst enemy. More's hatred for Tyndale and other reformers like Luther was fierce, and it filled his mind for much of his life.

More was speaker of the House of Commons, part of the English Parliament. He also had an important position at Cambridge University. In addition, he served as chancellor, or chief government officer, for the Duchy of Lancaster. But away from his public duties, in the privacy of his home, he wrote attacks against Protestant reformers. He declared that Tyndale's English translations were false and as "full of errors as the sea is of water." He even claimed the translations were the words of the devil:

> [Tyndale is] a hell-hound in the kennel of the devil ... discharging a filthy foam of his brutish beastly mouth.

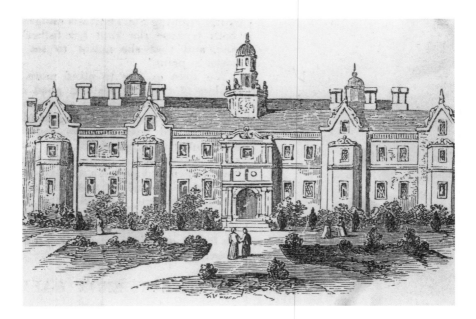

One of Thomas More's houses in England, where he spent his evenings writing attacks against Protestant reformers

He added that Tyndale intended to "deceive blind unlearned people." Thomas More and leaders of the Roman Catholic Church were upset about the words Tyndale used. But they were more concerned that the words were in English. More was afraid that once all English people read the Bible in their own tongue, a force might develop that church leaders could not control. He worried that a religious war might follow, which would harm the Catholic Church and England.

For several years, More and Tyndale debated each other in their writings. More charged that the reformers were committing treason. In 1528, Tyndale responded with the publication of *The Obedience of a Christian Man*. In 1529, More started writing against heresy in England and specifically against Tyndale and his work. In his *Dialogue Concerning Heresies,* More defended the Roman Catholic Church and voiced his hatred of Tyndale and Luther.

In 1530, More started encouraging Roman Catholic leaders to act more harshly against heretics. To him, the burning of heretics was right, lawful, and necessary, and he proceeded to carry out the punishment. A Catholic priest named Thomas Hitton was the first in England to be charged with heresy and sentenced to die. On February 23, 1530, Hitton was burned at the stake and became England's first martyr of the Protestant Reformation. More claimed that Hitton had learned his false faith and heresies from Tyndale's books.

A year after Hitton's death, Tyndale published *An Answer to Sir Thomas More's Dialogue*. In it he defended his English translation of the Bible and attacked what More had written in his *Dialogue Concerning Heresies*. He also wrote against the pope and religious ceremonies. In 1532, More replied back with his *Confutation of Tyndale*. More called Tyndale the "captain of English heretics" and claimed that he had united with Luther. But Tyndale denied the charge and kept on his own independent pathway to reformation.

Another powerful enemy of Tyndale's was Cardinal Wolsey. He had authority over all the Roman Catholic bishops around London, including Tunstall. Wolsey worked against Tyndale more behind the scenes, but he was determined to track him down and make him pay for his crime of heresy. In 1528, Wolsey ordered the arrest and delivery of Tyndale to authorities. He also ordered the burning of Tyndale's

Although he was a religious leader, Cardinal Thomas Wolsey (1475–1529) was the most powerful person in England after the king.

English Bibles and the arrest and punishment of many other reformers.

England's King Henry VIII also played an important part in Tyndale's life. The king wanted to break away from the Catholic Church, but his

During King Henry VIII's reign from 1509 to 1547, he had six wives, broke England's ties with the Roman Catholic Church, and closed down the monasteries in the country.

reasons were different from Tyndale's. He wanted to divorce his wife, Catherine of Aragon, but divorce was forbidden by the church.

It was customary for a king to turn over his throne to a son or male relative when he died. But since Catherine had not produced a son, Henry had no male heir. She had six pregnancies but only two children were born alive—a boy who lived less than two months and Mary.

Henry wanted to marry the much younger Anne Boleyn, one of his wife's beautiful ladies in waiting. Perhaps Anne would give him the son he had been wanting for so long. When Henry asked Pope Clement VII, the head of the Roman Catholic Church, to grant him a divorce, the pope refused.

Henry's daughter Mary (1516–1558) became Queen of England in 1553. She restored Catholicism as the official religion. For the next four years, she was responsible for about 300 Protestants being burned at the stake, which earned her the nickname "Bloody Mary."

Henry would not take no for an answer. In 1531, he established his own church—the Church of England—that was not under the pope's rule. He declared himself the head of this new national church. The Roman Catholic Church was not happy with Henry's decision. In fact, two years later, the church excommunicated him. The king himself was now banished from the church. But Henry didn't care—now he could divorce

King Henry VIII married Anne Boleyn after he divorced his first wife, Catherine of Aragon.

Catherine and marry Anne. Although Henry VIII was not against Catholicism, he was against the pope being so powerful. Many people criticized their king for trying to overrule the Roman Catholic Church. But an act of Parliament eventually proclaimed him the supreme head of the Church of England—a Protestant church.

Now that there was a new church in England, perhaps Tyndale would be safe there. Thomas Cromwell, the king's royal secretary, agreed with some of Tyndale's ideas and tried to persuade Henry to let Tyndale return to England under the king's protection and mercy. In early 1531, the king sent one of his agents, Stephen Vaughan, on a secret mission to find Tyndale.

At that time, Tyndale was in hiding in Antwerp, Belgium, but he must have heard that Vaughan was looking for him. He sent a messenger to Vaughan to say only that a friend wished to speak with him. The messenger then personally took Vaughan to meet Tyndale.

Tyndale told Vaughan he was upset that the king did not like his book titled *Prelates*. He also wanted the king to know how he had suffered greatly for his work on the Bible. He told Vaughan how he had been poor and exiled from his own country, away from his friends. He had suffered hunger, thirst, cold, and great danger as a fugitive.

Tyndale went on to ask how King Henry, a Christian, could dare say that it was not lawful for English people to have the Bible in their own language. Why were the people of England denied the Scriptures in a language they could understand?

Vaughan tried to persuade Tyndale to return to England with him, but Tyndale said he didn't feel safe. After all, some people might convince the king that promises made to heretics do not need to be kept. Vaughan met two more times with Tyndale, showing him a letter from Cromwell who believed the king would be "joyous" for Tyndale to return and that he would lean "to mercy, pity and compassion."

When Tyndale read Cromwell's letter, tears came

to his eyes, and he murmured, "What gracious words are these!" Tyndale was so moved by the invitation to return to his homeland that he proposed a deal with the king. He promised never to write again and to submit himself to the king, if only the Bible would

King Henry VIII receives a copy of an English Bible from his royal secretary, Thomas Cromwell.

be made available to the people of England in their own language.

King Henry was not totally against permitting an English Bible, but he was certainly not willing to do so just because Tyndale asked him to. The king and Tyndale did not come to an agreement, so Tyndale stayed in Antwerp and continued writing in exile. Tyndale later angered the king by speaking out against his divorce from Catherine and not supporting his marriage to Anne Boleyn. Tyndale said the Scriptures did not support divorce.

Tyndale would have liked to return to England in safety, but instead he chose to continue his lifelong project. He would translate and speak what he believed to be the truth, which would prove to be very dangerous. ❧

8 BURNED AT THE STAKE

After years of leading a hunted life throughout Europe, Tyndale finally settled in Antwerp, Belgium. Thomas Poyntz, the manager of a house there, was happy to give Tyndale shelter. Poyntz was related to the Walshes, for whom Tyndale had worked as a tutor in England. Tyndale shared the house with some English merchants, who even gave him money so he could continue to translate the Bible.

Tyndale spent his spare time doing charitable work. He helped the poor, the old, the weak, and the sick in Antwerp whenever he could. Those who knew him described him as a good, honest, and gentle man who had compassion for others.

Meanwhile, in England, a man named Henry Phillips and a monk named Gabriel Donne were hired to track down Tyndale. Their orders were to arrest

Antwerp, Belgium, was the last place William Tyndale lived.

him and bring him back to England, where he would be put to death as a heretic. Phillips and Donne came to Antwerp with the sole purpose of finding Tyndale and handing him over to the authorities.

Phillips pretended to be an elegant gentleman who agreed with the reformers, and Donne posed as Phillips' servant. When Phillips found Tyndale, they struck up an immediate friendship. They had similar

William Tyndale was born in England, but he spent many years of his life hiding out in cities throughout Europe.

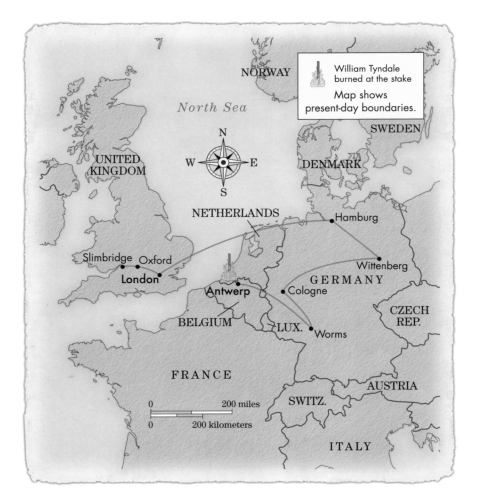

William Tyndale burned at the stake

Map shows present-day boundaries.

interests, including a flair for languages and a love of literature. Tyndale fell for the charm of this fellow Englishman.

On the evening of May 21, 1535, after agreeing to go out to dinner with Phillips, Tyndale unknowingly walked right into the hands of civil authorities and was immediately arrested. His rooms were searched, and all his possessions were seized. Because he was so well-known throughout Europe and was not an ordinary criminal, he was treated differently at first. He was allowed to eat dinner that evening before he was taken 18 miles (29 kilometers) to be imprisoned at the Castle of Vilvorde.

The castle, with its foreboding seven towers, a moat, and three drawbridges, was the main prison in the area. It was tightly secured and well-guarded. Inside, it was dark, damp, and smelly. Now Tyndale was treated like any other prisoner. He wasn't allowed to walk in the gardens or have anything delivered to him. He even had to pay for his own food.

Tyndale continued to write while he was in prison. His letters tell how much he suffered from the cold, the damp, and the darkness. But most of all, he wanted a copy of a Bible. In one of his letters, he wrote:

> [H]ave the kindness to send me ... a warmer cap; for I suffer greatly from cold in the head ... a warmer coat also, for this which I have is very thin. ... And I ask to

be allowed to have a lamp in the evening; it is indeed wearisome sitting alone in the dark. But most of all I beg ... that he will kindly permit me to have the Hebrew Bible, Hebrew grammar, and Hebrew dictionary, that I may pass the time in that study.

Although Tyndale's friends were doing everything they could to get him out of prison, there wasn't much chance he would be released. His friend Thomas Poyntz begged his brother John in a letter to obtain "the king's grace" to help Tyndale: "[I]n my conscience there be not many perfecter [more perfect] men living, as knows God."

His efforts, however, were useless. Tyndale remained in prison, and Thomas Poyntz was arrested for protecting Tyndale and agreeing with his teachings. Officials labeled Poyntz a heretic and questioned him. He refused to talk, which angered authorities more. They warned him that he would be condemned to death if he didn't speak up about what he knew. After about three months, Poyntz decided he would have to flee for his life.

Portrait of William Tyndale was most likely made after his death.

One evening in February 1536, Poyntz escaped from the house where he was being held and hid near the city gates of Brussels, Belgium. When the gates opened at dawn, he fled to the country and then to the coast. There, he boarded a boat and headed to England. He could never return to his home in Belgium. He lost his business, his property, and his family. His wife, who was not English, refused to come to England with their children. Poyntz had given up everything for his friend, William Tyndale.

Meanwhile, officials were questioning Tyndale about his beliefs and trying to convince him that he was wrong. One of the strongest charges against him was that he believed God granted salvation through faith in Jesus Christ. He refused to renounce his belief and would not support the position of the Roman Catholic Church that salvation comes through the church and by good works. Officials gave him many chances to change his mind, but he stood fast to what he believed.

In early August 1536, William Tyndale was found guilty of heresy. His position as a priest was taken away from him, and he was turned over to the authorities to be put to death. It was two months before the execution. Catholic priests tried to

Burning at the stake in public was used throughout Europe for more than 500 years (the 13th through the 18th centuries) to punish heresy and witchcraft. Strangling a person before the fire was lit was an act of mercy. But it was not the general practice to strangle heretics before they were burned. It was believed they should die a slow and horrible death. Burning was a preferred punishment because it didn't involve shedding of the victim's blood, which was not allowed by the Roman Catholic Church. It also ensured that the condemned had no body to take into the next life.

Lord ope the King of Englands eyes.

William Tyndale's last words before he was strangled were a prayer to God for the king of England.

persuade him to return to the beliefs of the Roman Catholic Church. Time and again, Tyndale refused, even though he knew that to do so sealed his fate.

On October 6, 1536, William Tyndale was bound and taken to a wooden stake that had been prepared for him. He was tied to the stake, strangled, and burned. This 42-year-old man who had dared to translate the New Testament into the English language was dead. But what he had accomplished did not die there at the stake. The spark of his convictions influenced many people for hundreds of years to come.

...ELMUS...   ...TUDEUS MARTYR

...EX...   AULA MAGD:

Hac ul luce tuas disperdam Roma tenebras
sponte ex torris ero sponte Sacrificium

9 INFLUENCE ON THE WORLD

ༀ

William Tyndale lost his life, but his dream came true—his dream that even "a boy that driveth the plough" shall know the Scriptures. Within two years of his death, Tyndale's dying prayer was answered. King Henry VIII gave permission for a version of the English Bible, based on Tyndale's work, to be used in England. Every man, woman, and child in England now had the opportunity to read or hear the Bible in English without fear of punishment or death.

Tyndale's efforts opened the door for his people to legally have the Bible in their own language. But his influence on the world was much greater. By producing and distributing a beautiful English version of the Bible, he helped to unify and create the English language as we know it today. His translation gave people the opportunity to be less dependent on the clergy. Now they could read and study the Bible on their own.

Almost 70 years after his death, Tyndale's Bible greatly influenced what would become the most well-known translation of the Holy Scriptures, the authorized King James Version. In 1604, England's King James I authorized a group of translators to begin working on a new version of the Bible for the English people. These men used various translations as a guide, but over and over, they chose Tyndale's words and phrases. In fact, about 80 percent of the King James Version of the Bible is actually from Tyndale's translation. His Bible was chosen for its beauty, style, and accuracy. His words and phrases are clearly present on every page.

The King James Version was finished and published in 1611. It became the best-selling translation of the Bible of all time. For hundreds of years, it has been read, heard, memorized, and quoted by millions of people. Many other versions of the Bible have been translated and printed since 1611, but the King James Version is the most familiar to English-speaking people all over the world.

Many of the now-familiar simple and timeless phrases came from Tyndale's translation—"eat, drink and be merry," "the salt of the earth," "judge not that ye be not judged," "greater love than this hath no man, than that a man bestow his life for his friends." These

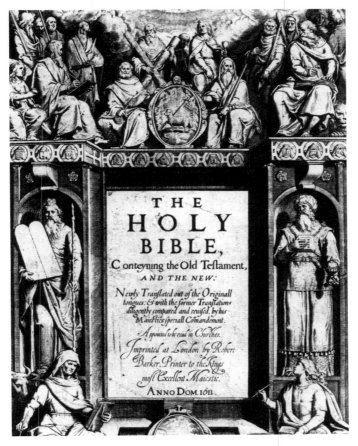

The authorized King James Version of the English Bible was completed in 1611.

phrases have remained almost unchanged. The Ten Commandments, as Tyndale translated them, are easy to recognize. Some of them read:

Honor thy father and mother,
*   that thy days may be long.*
Thou shalt not kill.
Thou shalt not steal.
Thou shalt bear no false witness
*   against thy neighbor.*

The people of England were very interested in Tyndale's English translation of the Bible.

Almost any part of the New Testament or the first five books of the Old Testament can be attributed to William Tyndale.

Tyndale also helped create a common language for England. Before the Bible was translated into English, many dialects of English were spoken. Often, people from different parts of England could not understand each other. Once the Bible was translated into English, nearly everyone was reading from the same translation in the same version of

English. Tyndale's version of the Bible became the standard for the English language. As people began to speak the language of the Bible, the English language became one language, and people could communicate better.

The way Tyndale wrote prose in the Bible became the style of the English language during the 1600s. Tyndale's English had rhythm, beauty, flow, and forcefulness. He wove the sounds and rhythms of the language into a poetic and musical-sounding text that could be understood by ordinary people. His style of writing influenced writers and poets, who were drawn to his simple, ordinary words. William Shakespeare, the famous 17th-century play-wright and poet, was greatly influenced by Tyndale's use of the English language. Shakespeare's writings are very similar to the language of Tyndale's Bible.

Tyndale's translation and religious writings also helped shape and expand the Protestant Reformation by changing the way people thought about religion.

The prose in Tyndale's English translation of the Bible influenced William Shakespeare's writings.

Tyndale helped carve out a new path of thinking about how people relate to God. His writings and translation clearly explained what the reformers believed. Through his words and teachings, Tyndale became an important leader of the Reformation.

William Tyndale was not the only one who believed strongly in the teachings of the Bible. He was not the only who lost his life for a cause he believed in during the Reformation. Many reformers were martyred for what they believed. Even Tyndale's greatest enemy, Sir Thomas More, suffered a violent death, although for a different reason.

On July 6, 1535, just six weeks after Tyndale was arrested, More was beheaded by order of the king of England. He had refused to support Henry VIII's marriage to Anne Boleyn. More never stopped supporting the pope, who had forbidden the king to divorce Catherine. For this, More's position in the English government was taken from him, and he was accused of treason. His headless corpse was given to his family for burial. But his head was displayed on a pole on London Bridge to terrorize and

John Foxe (1516-1587) was a 20-year-old college student in England when William Tyndale died. Throughout his life, Foxe was interested in the Protestants who were convicted of heresy and burned at the stake because they would not change their religious beliefs. In 1559, Foxe completed a written account of many of these people who chose to die a martyr's death. His book is commonly called Foxe's Book of Martyrs.

Sir Thomas More was executed at the Tower of London in 1535 for not supporting Henry VIII's divorce.

warn the citizens of England. The message was clear to all people: This is what happens to traitors.

Many years after More's death, the Roman Catholic Church honored him. He was officially recognized as a saint in 1935. Schools, colleges, streets, and monuments have since been named after St. Thomas More. His story was the subject of the play and 1966 film, *A Man for All Seasons.* On October 31, 2000, Pope John Paul II gave More the honor of being declared the patron saint of politicians.

But Tyndale has not received the same honors. Fewer schools, streets, and places are named after

The Vatican

Rome
Papal Gardens
Sistine Chapel (completed in 1483)
Basilica of St. Peter (completed in 1626)
St. Peter's Square (completed in 1667)
wall

Holy Roman Empire, 1500
Map shows present-day boundaries.

ICELAND

FINLAND

NORWAY
SWEDEN
ESTONIA RUSSIA
LATVIA
LITH.
RUS.
BELARUS

North Sea
DENMARK
Baltic Sea

IRELAND
UNITED KINGDOM
London
NETH.
BEL.
Wittenberg
POLAND
GERMANY

ATLANTIC OCEAN
CZECH REP.
Worms
UKRAINE
SLOVAKIA
LUX.
Basel
AUSTRIA HUNGARY
0   300 miles
0   300 kilometers
FRANCE
SWITZ.
ROMANIA
SLOV.
CRO.
ITALY
BOS. & HERZ.
SERB. & MONT.
BULGARIA
The Vatican (see inset)
Rome
MAC.
ALB.
PORTUGAL
SPAIN
GREECE

Mediterranean Sea

William Tyndale's English translation of the Bible helped spread the Reformation throughout Europe.

him. Statues and memorials in his honor are small and obscure. His life's work, however, triumphed and remains as a grand memorial to an important man who was willing to sacrifice his life for what he so fervently believed.

He believed people should turn to the Bible, not to

the church, as their only religious authority. Tyndale was convinced that it was each person's responsibility to read the Bible and privately discover the truths of God's Word. He believed those of humble origins had just as much right to pray and read the Bible as the clergy and the pope.

Tyndale once wrote:

> *As good is the prayer of a cobbler as of a cardinal, and of a butcher as of a bishop; and the blessing of a baker that knoweth the truth is as good as the blessing of our most holy father the pope.*

The writings and teachings of Tyndale still have a powerful effect on people. Many have embraced his belief that salvation comes only by faith in Jesus Christ. Others question whether the way to God is by private faith or through organized religion. Tyndale's work and his life have challenged people for hundreds of years.

Tyndale was not just a scholar and Bible translator. He was one of the creators of a unified English language and a significant leader of the Protestant Reformation. William Tyndale will long be remembered for the influence he had on religion and on the world. ☙

TYNDALE'S LIFE

C. 1494

Born near Slimbridge,
Gloucestershire,
England

1506

Attends Oxford
University in Oxford,
England

1500

1497

Vasco da Gama
becomes the first
western European
to find a sea route
to India

1503

Italian artist Leonardo
da Vinci begins painting
the *Mona Lisa*

WORLD EVENTS

1512

Graduates from
Oxford University
with a Bachelor of
Arts degree

1515

Receives a Master
of Arts degree from
Oxford University

1521

Ordained as a
priest in the Roman
Catholic Church

1520

1509

Henry, Prince of
Wales, at age 18,
becomes King
Henry VIII of
England

1517

Martin Luther posts
his *Ninety-Five Theses*
on the door of Castle
Church in Wittenberg,
beginning the Protestant
Reformation in Germany

TYNDALE'S LIFE

1522

Returns to
Gloucestershire,
England, to tutor
John Walsh's
children

1523

Announces his plan
to translate the Bible
into English

1524

Goes to Hamburg,
Germany, where he
begins translating the
New Testament

1522

Martin Luther finishes
translating the New
Testament into German

1524

German peasants rise
up against their land-
lords in the Peasants'
War, the greatest
mass uprising in
German history

WORLD EVENTS

1525

Flees to Worms,
Germany; prints
the English
New Testament

1526

Smuggles Bibles
into England

1525

Francis I is defeated
by Charles V, the Holy
Roman Emperor, at the
Battle of Pavia, Italy

1526

Oldest Protestant
university founded
at Liegnitz, Poland

1529

Moves to Antwerp, Belgium

1528

Publishes *The Obedience of a Christian Man*

1530

1529

Pope Clement VII refuses to grant England's Henry VIII a divorce, setting the stage for England's separation from the Roman Catholic Church

1528

Reformation begins in Scotland

WORLD EVENTS

1531

Publishes *An Answer to Sir Thomas More's Dialogue*

1535

Arrested and imprisoned at the Castle of Vilvorde in Belgium

1536

Convicted of heresy; strangled and burned at the stake October 6

1535

1534

Martin Luther completed translation of the Bible into German

1531

The "great comet," later called Halley's Comet, causes a wave of superstition

DATE OF BIRTH: c. 1494

ALSO KNOWN AS: William Tindal, Tindale, Tyndal and William Hutchins, Hychyns, Hutchyns, Hewchuns

BIRTHPLACE: Slimbridge, Gloucestershire, England

FATHER: Tindale (first name unknown)

MOTHER: name unknown

EDUCATION: Oxford University; Cambridge University

DATE OF DEATH: October 6, 1536

PLACE OF BURIAL: Ashes were thrown in the Senne River in Belgium

FURTHER READING

MacDonald, Fiona. *The Reformation (Events & Outcomes)*. Austin, Texas: Raintree Steck-Vaughn, 2003.

Mullet, Michael A. *The Reformation*. Crystal Lake, Ill.: Rigby Interactive Library, 1996.

Reformation and Enlightenment: Stories in History, 1500-1800. Boston: McDougal Littell, 2001.

Saari, Peggy, and Aaron Saari, eds. *Renaissance & Reformation Almanac*. Detroit, Mich.: UXL, 2002.

Shearer, Robert G. *Famous Men of the Renaissance and Reformation*. Lebanon, Tenn.: Greenleaf, 2000.

LOOK FOR MORE SIGNATURE LIVES BOOKS ABOUT THIS ERA:

Catherine de Medici: *The Power Behind the French Throne*
ISBN 0-7565-1581-5

Desiderius Erasmus: *Writer and Christian Humanist*
ISBN 0-7565-1584-X

Martin Luther: *Father of the Reformation*
ISBN 0-7565-1593-9

Pope Leo X: *Opponent of the Reformation*
ISBN 0-7565-1594-7

On the Web

For more information on *William Tyndale*, use FactHound.

1. Go to *www.facthound.com*
2. Type in a search word related to this book or this book ID: 0756515998
3. Click on the *Fetch It* button.

FactHound will find Web sites related to this book.

Historic Sites

Library of Congress
Thomas Jefferson Building,
North Great Hall Gallery
101 Independence Ave. S.E.
Washington, DC 20540
202/707-8000
On display is William Tyndale's 1526
pocket-sized edition of the New Testament
printed in Germany

The Huntington Library
1151 Oxford Road
San Marino, CA 91108
626/405-2100
On display is the fourth edition of
Tyndale's New Testament, secretly printed
in Antwerp, Belgium, in 1534

bishop
a spiritual leader in charge of the churches in a particular region

clergy
minister, priest, rabbi, or other person appointed to carry on religious work

communion
a Christian rite that honors Jesus' Last Supper, with clergy serving bread and wine

dialects
variations in a language

doctrine
set of religious beliefs

excommunicated
excluded from taking part in the church

exile
banishment from one's home country or area

heresy
opinion or belief that contradicts an established religious teaching

heretic
someone who spreads beliefs that contradict established religious teaching

Holy Scriptures
the sacred writings of the Bible divided into the Old Testament and New Testament

indulgences
official documents signed by the pope promising forgiveness of sins

linguist
someone who speaks several languages or finds it easy to learn languages

martyrs
people who give their lives for a worthy cause

ordained
appointed officially as a priest, minister, or rabbi

Protestants
members of Christian churches other than the Roman Catholic Church and Orthodox Church

recant
to withdraw something previously said

reformers
people who try to make a government or an organization more honest and efficient

renounce
to formally reject or give up a belief

tolerance
fairness toward people who hold different beliefs than one's own

translation
the changing of one language into another

translator
someone who changes written or spoken material from one language into another

Chapter 1

Page 10, line 9: David Daniell. *William Tyndale: A Biography.* London: Yale University Press, 1994, p. 364.

Page 14, line 15: Brian Moynahan. *God's Bestseller: William Tyndale, Thomas More, and the Writing of the English Bible—A Story of Martyrdom and Betrayal.* New York: St. Martin's Press, 2003, p. 376.

Page 15, line 2: Ibid., p. 378.

Chapter 4

Page 38, line 27: Ibid., p. 31.

Page 43, line 8: Ibid., pp. 51-52.

Chapter 5

Page 53, line 2: Ibid., p. 80.

Page 53, line 7: Ibid., p. 83.

Page 53, line 14: Ibid.

Chapter 6

Page 65, line 2: Benson Bobrick. *Wide as the Waters: The Story of the English Bible and the Revolution It Inspired.* New York: Penguin Books, 2001, p. 108.

Chapter 7

Page 68, line 22: *God's Bestseller,* p. 104.

Page 68, line 25: Ibid.

Page 69, line 1: Ibid.

Page 75, line 27: Ibid., p. 233.

Page 76, line 1: Ibid.

Chapter 8

Page 81, line 25: Ibid., p. 330.

Page 83, line 7: Ibid., p. 356.

Chapter 9

Page 88, line 25: Ibid., pp. 195.

Page 89, line 4: Ibid., pp. 195-196.

Page 95, line 8: Stephen P. Thompson. *The Reformation.* San Diego, Calif.: Greenhaven Press, 1999, p. 222.

Bobrick, Benson. *Wide as the Waters: The Story of the English Bible and the Revolutiuon It Inspired.* New York: Penguin Books, 2001.

Bridgman, Joan. "Tyndale's New Testament." *Contemporary Review,* 277.1619 (2000): 342-346.

Cahill, Elizabeth Kirkland. "A Bible for the Plowboy: Tyndale at the New York Public Library." *Commonweal,* 124.7 (1997): 19-20.

Daniell, David. *William Tyndale: A Biography.* London: Yale University Press, 1994.

Hart, Jeffrey. "Burn, Tyndale, Burn." *National Review,* 49.19 (1997): 74-77.

Hillerbrand, Hans Joachim. *The World of the Reformation.* New York: Scribner, 1973.

"Let There Be Light." *The Economist (US),* 330.7846 (1994): 92.

Lindberg, Carter. *The European Reformations.* Oxford: Blackwell Publishers, 1996.

MacCulloch, Diarmaid. *The Reformation.* New York: Viking, 2003.

McGrath, Alister E. *In the Beginning: The Story of the King James Bible and How It Changed a Nation, a Language, and a Culture.* New York: Anchor Books, 2001.

Moynahan, Brian. *God's Bestseller: William Tyndale, Thomas More, and the Writing of the English Bible—A Story of Martyrdom and Betrayal.* New York: St. Martin's Press, 2003.

Nicolson, Adam. *God's Secretaries: The Making of the King James Bible.* New York: HarperCollins, 2003.

Pill, David H. *The English Reformation 1529-58.* Totawa, N.J.: Rowman and Littlefield, 1973.

Timothy, George. "The Translator's Tale." *Christianity Today,* 38.12 (1994): 36-39.

"Tyndale's New Testament Visits America." *U.S. News & World Report,* 121.20 (1996): 12.

Fran Rees is the author of children's educational books and books on team leadership and group communication. She has taught English and music at the elementary and junior high school levels. She keeps extensive written and art journals of her life and interests. She lives in Mesa, Arizona, with her husband and daughter.

Image Credits